# FAT CATS

# FAT

# RITZ

 **HARPER & ROW, PUBLISHERS**, New York
Cambridge, Philadelphia, San Francisco, London, Mexico City, São Paulo, Sydney

# CATS

## BY TERRY DEROY GRUBER

FAT CATS. Copyright © 1981 by Terry deRoy Gruber. All rights reserved. Printed in the United States of America. No part of this book may be used or reproduced in any manner whatsoever without written permission except in the case of brief quotations embodied in critical articles and reviews. For information address Harper & Row, Publishers, Inc.,10 East 53rd Street, New York, N.Y. 10022. Published simultaneously in Canada by Fitzhenry & Whiteside Limited, Toronto.

FIRST EDITION

Designer: Gai Moseley

**Library of Congress Cataloging in Publication Data**

Gruber, Terry deRoy.
    Fat cats.

    (Harper colophon book)
    1. Cats — Pictorial works. I. Title.
SF446.G77   636.8'0022'2   81-47086
ISBN 0-06-090897-1 (pbk.)   AACR2

81 82 83 84 85 10 9 8 7 6 5 4 3 2 1

# To Mom & Dad
and the rest of the litter

# Acknowledgments

*Assistants:* Carol Klebanow, Ellen McManmon

*Project Editor:* Lawrence P. Ashmead

*Chief Editorial Assistant:* Marnie Goodman

*Additional Editorial Assistance:* Grace Anderson, Julian Blau, Joanna Bobrowicz, Pam Brown, Ellen Davis, Jon Davis, Anne Dayton, Marlaina Deppe, Emily Greenspan, Warren Leight, George Marvin, Craig Nelson, Peter Oliver, Jon Ross, Lenny Russ, Tony Sherer, Jennifer Smith, Ron Stone, Wesley Strick, Gwen Wattenberg

*Photo Editor:* Nancy Buirski

*Darkroom:* Michel Gardere, Vito Gianganspero (Fashion Lab), Paul Phillips

*Black & White Prints:* Mike Levins

*Book Design:* Gai Moseley

Thank you: Jane Ubell, *Good Morning America*; George Frazier, *Independent Journal*, Marin, CA; Dick Lochtee, LA *Times*; Anne Germain, *Monterey Peninsula Herald*; Allene Arthur, *Desert Sun*, Palm Springs, CA; Jane Marshall, Fort Worth *Star Telegram*; Life Style Editor, New Orleans *Times Picayune*; Colleen Fahey, Daniel J. Edelman Associates.

And special thanks to Anitra, Stephen Green-Armytage, Ilze Brunas, Riker Davis, Steve Herman, Debbie Maguire, Kate Neiswender, Mike Singer, Dr. and Mrs. Peter Tynberg, David Wagner, Caryn Weiss, and all the key people in New York, California, Nevada, Arizona, New Mexico, Texas, Tennessee and Kentucky too numerous to mention who devoted their time and extended their hospitality to me for this project.

**făt căt** (făt′kăt; F, *făt chăt′*) *n* **1**: Facile, faddish, famous, fancy, fashionable feline (species *Fatus Catus*) **2 a**: Fatalist **b**: Faultless **3**: Favorite featured felon (e.g., Catsy Malone) **4**: Ferocious, feminine, fetching, fetishist **5**: Fickle, finagling, finicky, first-class, first-rate flabby (often construed as a pancake) **6**: Flawless fledgling (as in "My Suzy would never do a thing like that") *syn slang* DAP: Domesticated American Princess) **7**: Fluffy **8 a**: Flush, foolhardy, footloose, foreigner (exclusive: Burmese, Siamese, Persian, etc.) **b**: Formidable, fortunate, four-legged freelancer **9**: Free-thinking, free-willed, frolicsome fussbudget (*ant* Working Cat) **10**: Full, fulfilled, full-blown, full-time (times nine), furry, fussy, fuzzy

# Möet & Chandon

We spend much of our time pondering the difference between illusion and reality.

# Veronica Lake

I'm ready for my close-up now, Mr. De Mille.

# Veronica Lake

I'm ready for my close-up now, Mr. De Mille.

# Hunk

Who said it's lonely at the top?

# Lillian

What becomes a legend most?

# Rhett & Ashley

There's a man at the door with 75 pounds of crab?
Now who could have ordered that?

# Fat Black

Dear Terry:

I own an advertising agency in Palm Springs. I tell my clients they can't lose: if the ad doesn't work, I'll send my 29-pound cat out to maul the competition.

# Cosmo

Darling, have you ever seen such deco?

## Cat Walder III

But I always leave the spare key up here.

# Peanut

Can you find *moi* in this picture?

27

# Suzy

Do Not Disturb.

# Max

What could be more purr-fect than living
in the best little cathouse in Nevada.

## Pixie Star, Dixie Star Tenschi, & Mike Neko Sakura

Don't look at us—we didn't do the decorating.

## Love Bucket Smith aka LBS.

We all must conquer our little piece of world.

# Kong

I believe you're sitting
in my favorite chair.

# Nefertiti & Tutankhamen

Let's go places and eat things.

# Gloria

I'm not coming in till she leaves.

# Pooh Pooh La Rue

"Diet" is not only a four-letter word. It's distasteful.

# Pierre & Badaustin

Social climber!

# Dominique

Seulement ma styliste sait pour sûr.*

*Only my hairdresser knows for sure.

## Spicey

The calla lilies are in bloom again.

# Velvet

Oh, look, Jack has his martini flag up.

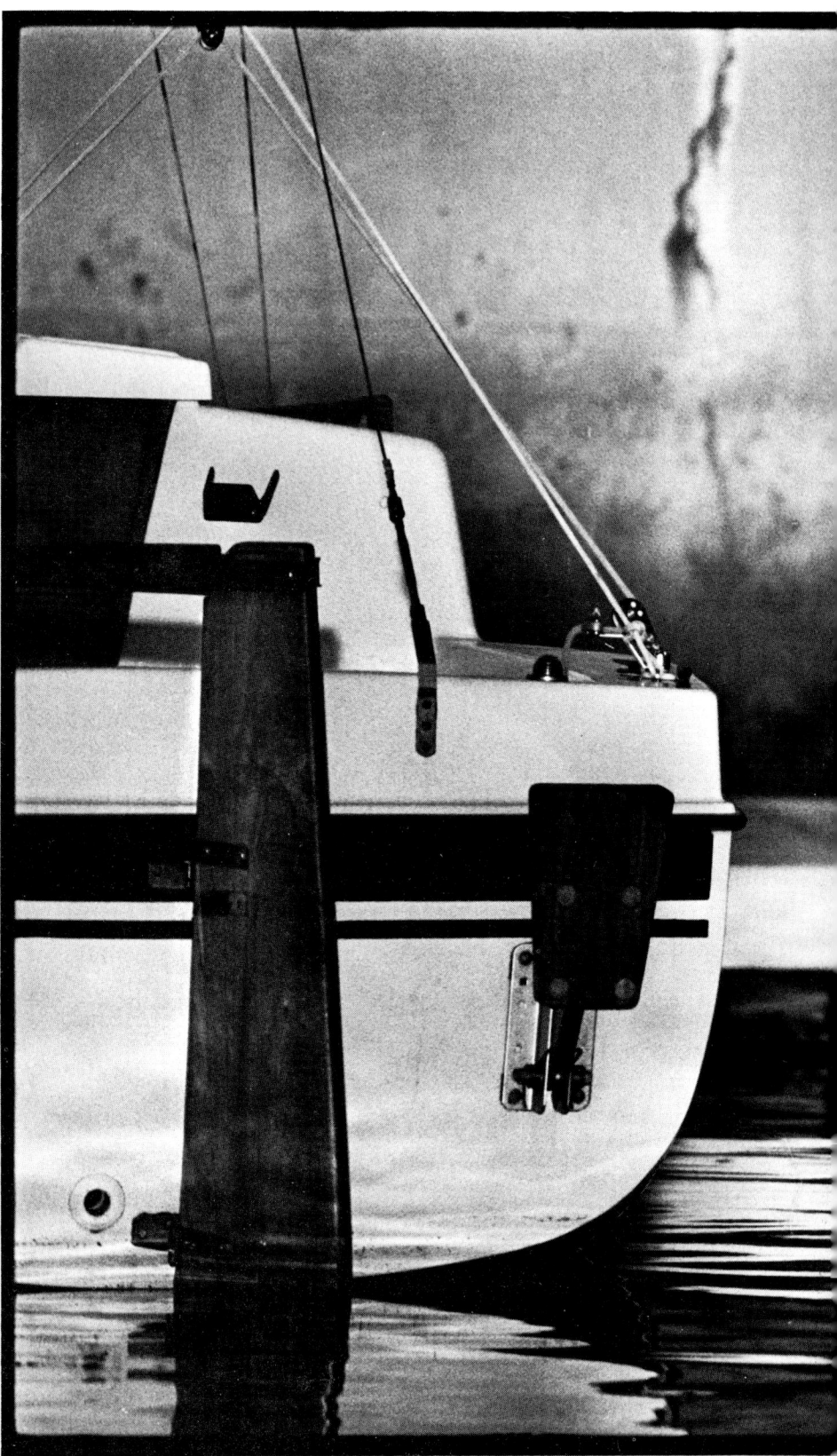

# Sheldon

Excuse me, but can you direct me to a good re-tailer?

# Alex & Annie

I hope she doesn't expect too much after this workout.

# Leo

And all this is mine.

## J.R.

I'd prefer to be in oil.

# Tyrone Power

My owner lost a bundle at the dog races. I thought everyone knew dogs were a bad bet.

# Mutt & Jeff

I know a lot of folks who live in this neighborhood think the only reason I come around every night to make sure these cats get fed is because they're all I have in the world. I wonder how many realize I'm all they have in the world.

*Mrs. Pauline Manning*

# Princess Daisy Mann

Of course, I was younger then . . .

# Sparky

*!%?#... They told me this stuff would only last for six hours ...

# Linus

When a Rolls purrs, people listen.

# Doc

Frank Langella, eat your heart out.

# April Fluff

Happiness is living at Dairy Queen headquarters.

# Margie

I *said* no more autographs!

## Alfred

Charles, prepare my chat-longue.

## YSL & Zza Zza

Look carefully. You will never again see perfection.

# Morris the Cat<sup>®</sup>

One thing for you beginners to remember:
never seem too eager.

# Clea

How would I define minimalism? Obviously, it's a way of decorating intended to best show off one's cat.

# Sugar

Dear Mr. Gruber:

This is Sugar. All the residents and employees of our home think she is special and believe me, Sugar *knows* she is special. She has an RN to give her her shots, an Administrator to buy her food, and everyone else to feed and pamper her whenever she wants.

I know the residents would be so proud if Sugar were in *Fat Cats*, but as far as Sugar is concerned, I am sure she could care less.

*Betty Dean, Bookkeeper*

# Humbert Humbert

Ay, there's the rub.

# Lover

Anybody for the Canary Islands?

# Miss Missy

What?! A mouse in *this* house? Why, the very idea!

## Nappy & Josephine

Of course, Vienna isn't what it was before the war...

# Duke

She's only Miss January. *I'm* the Pet-of-the-Year.

# Christina

Photograph? I deserve to be in a *painting*.

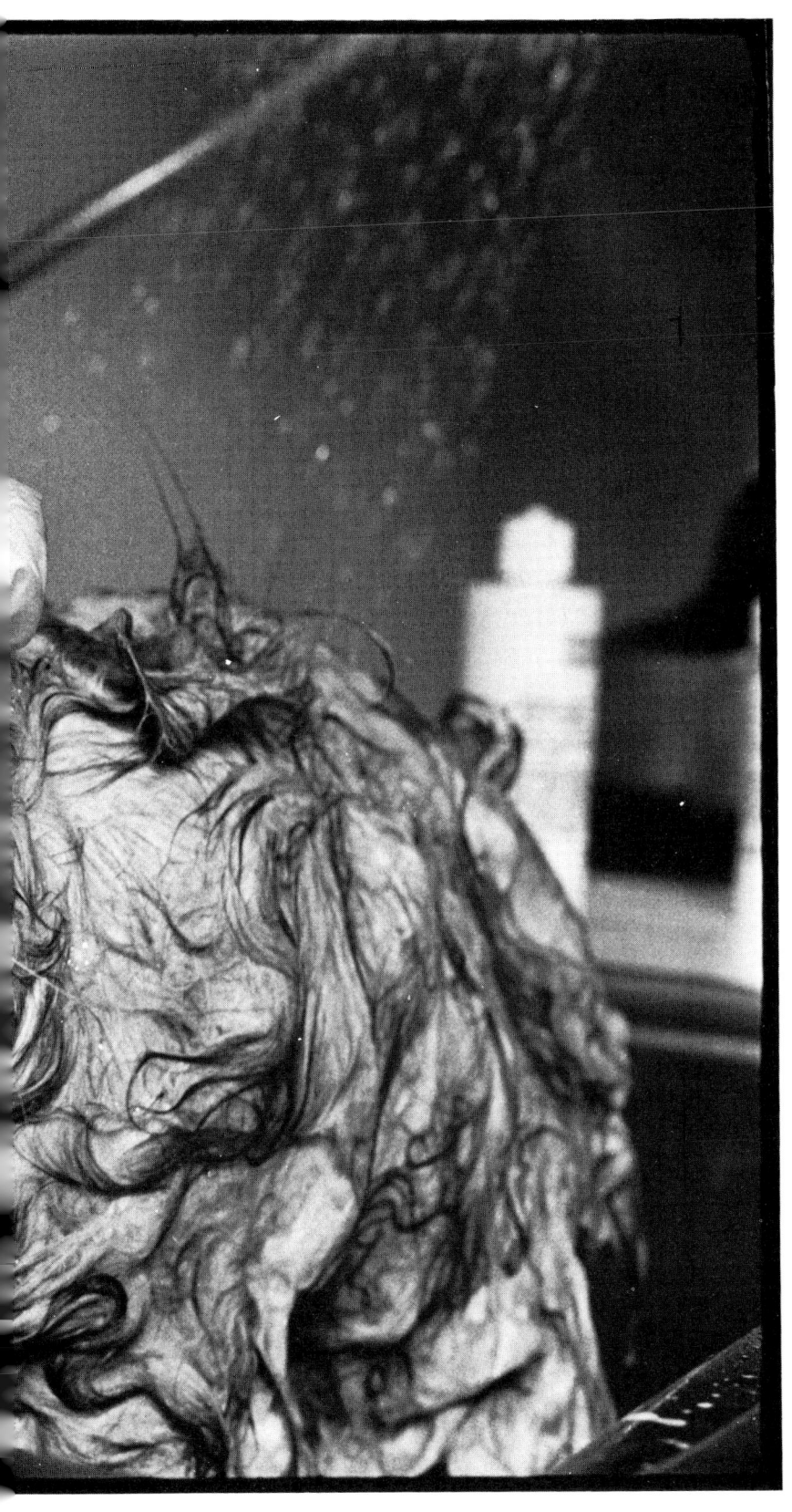

# Betty-Sue

I don't want a *tight* perm,
just something soft, wavy,
and maybe a little henna, or
some highlights in the nape,
but ... what do you think?

# Oliver

Ever since that German shepherd moved in next door,
we decided good fences really do make good neighbors.

# Epi

My beauty is far more than skin deep . . .

# Topaz

On my left you'll notice a King Edward settee given to Mrs. Moore by the Duke of Wales; behind that is my own eighteenth-century Regency litterbox.

# Me-Too & You-Who

It's amazing what the right haircut can do for you.

# George

It's not New York but it's better for my asthma.

## The Katzes
with Moe at center

I told a friend,
and she told a friend,
and so on,
and so on,
and so on ...

## Mr. Tudball

Trust me.

# Kouska

Mirror, mirror on the wall . . .

# Fastbuck

I offer you my foot in matrimony . . . if you agree to sign a prenuptial agreement.

# Tai

I'm not just another loafer.

# F. Scott

I have the most curious feeling of solitude and multitude.

# Big Cat

In my circle of acquaintances, the expression goes: "You can never be too rich or too fat."

# Blackie

Reports of my death have been grossly exaggerated.

# Niki

I know I shouldn't have eaten that last tuna croquette.

# Raccoon Kitty & Elizabeth

Dear Terry,

We have a large, cross-eyed, haughty cat called Raccoon Kitty. Although he is short in stature, he is <u>large</u> in bulk. I love him very much and know he would make a valuable contribution to your book. I've included some impurrrrfect photos.

Sincerely,
Elizabeth Green

P.S. He weighs about 15 pounds.

# Ping Ping & Pong Pong

Shh—I think I hear someone coming.
Better put back that jewelry.

## Charpurr's Brooke of Cosmos

I'm not insecure about my ears.
Cats are notoriously bad listeners.

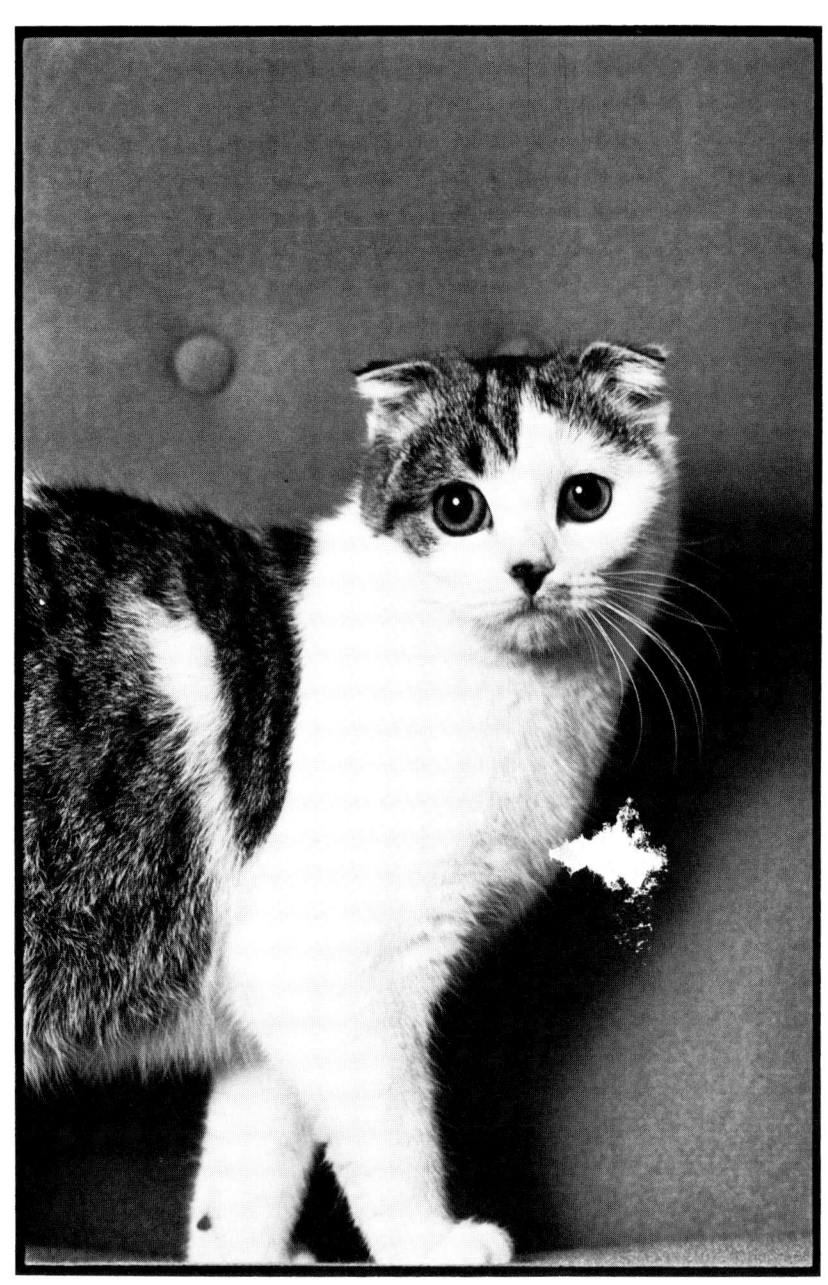

# Everest

What's a pedigree
without the family tree?

# Sasha

It's downright catlike.

# Larry

I love the space but the upkeep is killing me.

# Julian

They call it high-tech. I call it boring.

# Sergeant

That mouse is too small by itself,
but maybe it has a family . . .

## Unnamed Cat

I vant to be a lawn . . .

## Bijou Jamala of Sylabee & Guests

*At* six? I could have sworn you said dinner *for* six!

# Grey Cat

I'm sort of stuck on stucco.

# Tosca

Just when I lost the urge for paté, I discovered the imported cheeses.

## J.C.

Veni, vidi, vici.

# Snoopy

I don't know how I ever lived without cable.

# Talese

*I'm* the author's cat.

# Whitey

Oh, dear.
And I so wanted
a Longines ...

Next stop Grauman's Chinese.